The Great Nevada FOOD FESTIVAL Cookbook

By Richard Moreno

Illustrated by April Pedersen

A NEVADA MAGAZINE COOKBOOK

Copyright © 1997 by Nevada Magazine. All rights reserved.
Nevada Magazine, 1800 Hwy. 50 East, Suite 200, Carson City, NV 89701-3202 • (702) 687-5416

INTRODUCTION

Nevada is home to hundreds of events ranging from Basque festivals to harvest fairs. Food plays an integral role in many of those events. In some cases, such as the Best in the West Nugget Rib Cook-Off, eating is the event's *raison d'être*. In others, food is an important side dish to music and dance and other activities.

The ***Great Nevada Food Festival Cookbook*** is a celebration of the state's food-related special events. With such a cornucopia of culinary affairs, it was natural that the editors of ***Nevada Magazine*** collect some of the unique recipes associated with the state's various food festivals.

You can enjoy the award-winning recipe by Dr. Chili (Dr. Ed Pierczynski of Carson City) that won him the 1992 World Championship Chili Cook-Off. Also revealed is the famous fudge recipe from the Genoa Candy Dance, which is held each September in Nevada's oldest community. For more adventurous palates, there are tips from Dennis Ofsthun, winner of the 1996 Best in the West Nugget Rib Cook-Off, on barbecuing ribs and a recipe for eggplant lasagna with mini veal meatballs from the Eldorado Hotel, host of Reno's Great Italian Festival. In honor of Cinco de Mayo, we snuck in a ringer—our own Isabel Espinoza's family recipe for biscochitos.

With so many food-related special events held throughout the state, we couldn't include every one of them. For a complete, updated listing of all special events, please refer to the ***Nevada Events and Shows*** section in every issue of ***Nevada Magazine***. This cookbook is dedicated to everyone who has ever ladled spaghetti sauce, baked cookies, marinated steaks, stirred chili, or flipped pancakes at a food event.

Richard Moreno
Publisher, Nevada Magazine

Special note: Common cooking abbreviations are used in recipes; e.g.: lbs. for pounds, oz. for ounces, tsp. for teaspoon, and Tbsp. for tablespoon.

CONTENTS

Chili Cook-Offs 6

Greek Food Festival 8

Cinco de Mayo 10

Italian Festivals 13

Genoa Candy Dance 16

Basque Festivals 18

Japan Festival 22

Rib Cook-Offs 24

Portuguese Festas 26

Cranberry Festival 28

CHILI COOK-OFFS

Creating taste bud-torching chili is pursued with religious fervor in some parts of Nevada. Every year, more than a dozen championship chili cook-offs are conducted throughout the state, including the World's Championship Chili Cook-Off, held in early October at the Reno Hilton.

Most chili cook-offs are sanctioned by the International Chili Society. The ICS guidelines are simple—avoid seeds, floating fat, alcohol, and stringy meats, and never use beans or chunks of vegetables. It is perfectly all right, however, to incorporate exotic meats (buffalo and deer occasionally are used) as well as tomatoes, celery, onions, peppers, and any spices.

Of course, merely following the general rules doesn't guarantee championship chili. Within those seemingly narrow parameters are infinite possibilities, which is what making a good batch of chili is all about.

The first recipe is courtesy of Dr. Ed Pierczynski of Carson City, who cooked his way to the world championship in 1992, while the second, contributed by Tom Bender of Dayton, has won praise at the annual Carson City Chili Cook-Off, held in October.

DOC'S SECRET REMEDY

3 lbs. cubed or course ground sirloin or tri-tip
6 oz. sausage (Italian, spicy or otherwise)
2 14-1/2 oz. cans beef broth
8-oz. can of Hunt's tomato sauce
6-oz. can of Snap-E-Tom tomato juice
11 Tbsp. Gebhardt chili powder
1 tsp. garlic powder
1 Tbsp. onion powder
1 Tbsp. cumin
2 tsp. Tabasco pepper sauce
Salt to taste

Saute beef. Fry sausage until done and drain well. Place beef, sausage, and one-half can of beef broth in chili pot and bring to a slow simmer. Add 8 oz. can of tomato sauce, Snap-E-Tom, 6 Tbsp. of Gebhardt chili powder, 1 tsp. of garlic powder, 1 Tbsp. of onion powder, 1 tsp. of Tabasco pepper sauce. Simmer slowly for about an hour and 30 minutes or until meat is tender. Add the remaining 5 Tbsp. of Gebhardt chili powder, 1 tsp. of cumin, and 1 tsp. Tabasco pepper sauce. Simmer for 30 minutes. Salt to taste. This prescription is good for what ails ya! It is known to cure lumbago, mange, dry rot, blind staggers, and a bad hangover. As a precaution for those stomach burners, keep something to prevent acid reflux handy. This will serve 6 to 8 hungry interns.

COMPUTER BASE HARDRIVIN' CHILI

Stuff you'll need:

hamburger	Yerington garlic
pork sausage	Hatch, New Mexico green chile
red beans	jalapeños
pinto beans	red chili powder
tomato sauce	crushed red pepper
tomatoes	beer
onions	salt and pepper
bell peppers	

Soak beans overnight, then season and boil. Brown hamburger and sausage with some onions and chile powder, salt and pepper. In a large pot, bring tomato sauce and chopped vegetables to a simmer. Add browned meat, cooked beans, and beer. Add spices to taste. Drink remaining beer. We could tell you what proportions to use, but that would take the fun out of it. Just make it up as you go along—it worked for us.

GREEK FOOD FESTIVAL

Since 1972, Las Vegas has celebrated its Greek community's rich heritage and traditions at the annual Greek Food Festival, held in May. The festival is a fund-raiser for the St. John's Greek Orthodox Church in Las Vegas. In addition to Greek dancing and music, the event features a feast of Greek dishes ranging from baklava pastries to spanakopita (spinach squares).

The following recipes are courtesy of the Las Vegas Greek Food Festival.

DOLMATHES
(Stuffed Grape Leaves)

1 jar grapevine leaves
2 lbs. lean ground beef
1 cup short grain rice
1 tsp. dill weed
1/2 tsp. cumin
1 large onion diced
1/2 cup vegetable oil
2 cups chicken broth or water
Salt and pepper to taste

Place meat into large bowl and add diced onion (onion can be sauteed in oil if desired). Add salt, pepper, dill weed, cumin, oil, and mix well. Add rice and 1/2 cup water. Mix by hand until blended together. Place about 1 Tbsp. of mixture in center of washed leaf (ribbed side up) and roll into narrow roll. Place rolls into deep saucepan in layers. Add chicken broth, cover, and simmer about 45 minutes over low heat until rice is done.

SHISH KEBAB

5-7 lbs. leg of lamb
1/2 cup (1/4 lb.) butter
1/2 cup olive oil
1 cup fresh lemon juice
2 Tbsp. oregano
1/2 tsp. pepper
10-12 medium tomatoes, quartered
5-6 medium onions, quartered and seperated
5-6 green peppers, cut into 2-inch pieces
8-10 15-inch skewers (double-pronged are recommended)

It is preferable to have a butcher cut lamb into cubes. Place lamb cubes in a deep bowl. Melt butter with oil, lemon, oregano, and pepper. Pour over lamb cubes. Marinate 4-5 hours at room temperature. Skewer lamb, onions, tomatoes, and peppers in that order. Roast over hot coals or broil. Baste constantly with the remaining marinade. Turn skewers frequently for even cooking. Serve on a bed of rice pilaf. The same marinade is excellent for lamb chops, too.

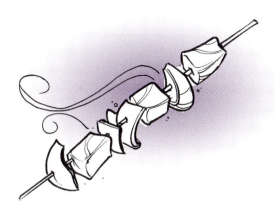

CINCO DE MAYO

Cinco de Mayo (May 5th) celebrations commemorate the 1862 Battle of Puebla, an important strategic victory in Mexico's long struggle for independence. While often mistaken for Mexican Independence Day, which is September 16, Cinco de Mayo is celebrated for its symbolic importance as the date that Mexican forces defeated a better-equipped European enemy (the French) and began their country's drive for self determination and national sovereignty.

In Nevada, Cinco de Mayo celebrations are held throughout the state, including well-attended festivals in Las Vegas and Sparks. These events can often include exhibitions of traditional Mexican dancing, mariachi and country-western norteño music, parades, Latin arts and crafts, and plenty of food.

The following recipes are courtesy of Isabel Espinoza, **Nevada Magazine's** retail coordinator, and Garduño's Chile Packing Company, located in the Fiesta Hotel-Casino, 2400 North Ranch Drive, North Las Vegas.

BISCOCHITOS

6 cups flour
1/4 tsp. salt
3 tsp. baking powder
2 cups lard or 1-1/2 cups butter
1-1/2 cups sugar
2 tsp. anise seeds
2 eggs
1/4 cup brandy
1 Tbsp. cinnamon (as needed)

Cream lard or butter and sugar together, then beat in eggs one at a time. Add anise seeds. Sift flour, baking powder, and salt and add to mixture, along with the brandy, and mix until well blended. Roll out on floured board to about 3/8-inch thickness. Cut into shapes. Dust with a mixture of sugar and cinnamon. Bake at 350 degrees F for 10 minutes or until golden brown.

GAZPACHO

1/4 lb. day-old Italian or French bread, cubed
1 quart water
1-1/2 cups cucumber, pared and diced
1 medium green pepper, seeded and cut up
1 or 2 cloves garlic
2 tsp. salt
1/2 cup olive oil
1/4 cup wine vinegar
2 lbs. fresh ripe tomatoes, seeded and cubed

Place bread in shallow dish; add water 1-inch deep. Let bread soak, turning once. Meanwhile, combine cucumber, green pepper, garlic, salt, oil, and vinegar in electric blender and blend smooth. Add half of the bread and blend smooth. Pour into a bowl. Blend remaining bread and tomatoes and add to mixture in bowl. Chill thoroughly. When ready to serve, place 1 or 2 ice cubes in each bowl of soup. Serve with an accompaniment. Accompaniments can be diced or thin slices of cucumber, chopped scallions or onions, or sliced toasted almonds.

GARDUÑO'S HATCH GREEN CHILE STEW

1/2 cup vegetable oil
2 lbs. beef stew meat
1 tsp. black pepper
1/2 tsp. garlic, granulated
1 cup bell pepper, diced
1 cup onions, diced
3-1/4 cups Hatch green chile, diced (This is a type of pepper grown in Hatch, N.M. If not available, substitute green chile of choice)
1-1/2 cups carrots, cut into 1/2-inch slices
2 lbs. cubed potatoes

(Continued)

1 Tbsp. beef base (or use 1 bouillon cube)
2 cups green chile sauce
2 cups tomatoes, diced
2 Tbsp. corn starch mixed with 1/2 cup of cold water

Heat oil in large skillet. Add stew meat, black pepper, garlic, and salt. Sauté until meat is well-browned and cooked medium-well. Add bell peppers, onion, green chile, and carrots. Sauté with meat until onion is transparent, about 5 minutes. Drain excess oil. Add beef bouillon cube, potatoes, water, green chile sauce, and diced tomatoes. Bring to a rolling boil for 15 minutes. Add corn starch mixed with cold water, reduce heat, and simmer for an additional half-hour, stirring occasionally. Serve piping hot with warm flour tortillas.

ITALIAN FESTIVALS

Grape stomping, jugglers, mimes, gelato-eating contests, pasta feeds, and spaghetti sauce cook-offs highlight Italian Festivals held every October in Reno and Las Vegas. The events, which celebrate Columbus Day, have become unofficial Italian-American Heritage Days. Reno's Great Italian Festival is held at the Eldorado Hotel while the Las Vegas Italian Festival takes place at the Rio Suite Hotel.

The following recipes are courtesy of the Carano family, owners of the Eldorado Hotel, and the Rio Suite Hotel.

ELDORADO HOTEL'S RISOTTO AL FUNGHI SELVATICI
(Rice with Wild Mushrooms)

1 lb. rice "carnaroli" or "arbori"
10 oz. wild mushrooms: shiitake, portobello, or oyster
34 fluid oz. chicken stock
1 tsp. fresh chopped garlic
1 Tbsp. fresh chopped onion
3 Tbsp. butter
4 Tbsp. fresh grated parmesan cheese
1 Tbsp. fresh chopped Italian parsley

Clean and cut the mushrooms into large pieces. Sauté onion and garlic in a sauce pan. Add mushrooms and rice with 1/3 of the hot chicken stock. Cook the rice until the liquid evaporates and add 1/3 hot chicken stock and repeat. The rice needs 18 minutes to cook. When the rice is cooked remove from the stove and add butter, parmesan cheese, and parsley. Stir the rice until the butter is melted.

(Continued)

ELDORADO HOTEL'S LASAGNA CON MELANZANE E POLPETTINE

(Eggplant Lasagna with Mini Veal Meatballs)

2 medium eggplants, diced
1 Tbsp. garlic, chopped
1 Tbsp. onion, onion
1 Tbsp. oregano, chopped
1 Tbsp. basil, chopped
4 lbs. Roma tomatoes, diced
1 lb. mozzarella cheese, shredded
2 boxes lasagna noodles

For mini meatballs:
1 lb. ground veal
1 tsp. garlic, chopped
1 Tbsp. ground parmesan cheese
salt and pepper to taste

Preparation: Start to make mini meatballs. Mix all the ingredients together and form small (size of a quarter) balls. Put meatballs in a baking pan and place pan in an oven preheated to 350 degrees for 15 minutes. For the sauce: Sauté garlic, onions, and the herbs. Add eggplant, salt and pepper, and tomatoes and cook for 30 minutes. For the lasagna: Cook lasagna noodles in salted, boiling water "al dente." Remove noodles. Rinse in cold water and lay noodles flat to dry. In casserole dish layer noodles, sauce, mini meatballs, mozzarella, and repeat four times. Finish final layer with rest of mozzarella. Bake in 350-degree oven until cheese is gratinated.

THE RIO'S MARINARA SAUCE

1/2 cup olive oil
1 large white onion chopped fine
1 stalk celery chopped fine
1 peeled carrot chopped fine
1 Tbsp. whole dry basil

1/2 Tbsp. whole dry oregano
1/2 Tbsp. whole dry marjoram
2 Tbsp. chopped garlic
2 16-oz. cans diced tomato (do not drain)
1 Tbsp. salt
1 tsp. white pepper
1-1/2 Tbsp. white sugar
1 4-oz. can tomato paste
4-6 anchovy filets (optional)

Sauté onion, celery, carrot, garlic, marjoram, basil, and oregano in olive oil over medium heat for 5-6 minutes. Add remaining ingredients and simmer on low heat for 15-20 minutes, stirring periodically on slow boil. For a thinner sauce, you can add tomato juice or V-8 juice to your liking.

THE RIO'S HOT ITALIAN SAUSAGE

5 lbs. coarse ground pork butts
1 Tbsp. salt
1-1/2 Tbsp. fennel seeds (soaked in water overnight)
1 Tbsp. paprika
1 tsp. black pepper
1 tsp. cayenne pepper
1/2 tsp. crushed red chilies

Mix all ingredients well and let sit overnight for fuller flavor. Cook thoroughly when ready to use.

GENOA CANDY DANCE

One of Nevada's oldest special events is the Genoa Candy Dance, which has been held nearly every year since 1919 in the state's first permanent settlement. The September event is a unique fund-raiser for the tiny hamlet of Genoa, which uses proceeds to pay for maintaining street lights, streets, the town park, and other community needs.

The Candy Dance includes a popular three-day craft festival with nearly 300 booths, a turkey-and-ham buffet dinner, a community dance, and thousands of pounds of candy for sale.

The Genoa Divinity recipe is courtesy of Libby Crouse and Maria Meyer-Kassel of Genoa. The Genoa Candy Dance Fudge is courtesy of Thelma Schenk of Genoa and Lisa Lekumberry of Minden.

GENOA DIVINITY

4 cups sugar
1 cup white Karo syrup
1 cup cold water
4 egg whites, stiffly beaten
1 tsp. vanilla
1 cut nutmeats

Boil first three ingredients rapidly until they form a firm but not real hard ball (260 degrees) when tested in cold water. Slowly beat mixture into the egg whites. Add vanilla and nutmeats at very last. Drop by teaspoons on waxed paper and let stand until firm.

GENOA CANDY DANCE FUDGE

You'll need:
Large sheet cake/cookie type tray
Waxed butcher paper

Set aside in a large bowl:
24 oz. (1-1/2 bags) marshmallows
6 cups (54 oz.) semi-sweet chocolate chips
3 cups walnut pieces (optional)
Combine:
3 12-oz. cans evaporated milk
6 cubes (1-1/2) lbs. margarine
15 cups sugar
6 Tbsp. Karo corn syrup

Bring milk, margarine, sugar, and corn syrup to a boil, stirring constantly. Cook to a soft ball stage (231 degrees). Remove from heat. Pour over marshmallow-chocolate chip mixture and beat with spoon until it loses its gloss. Pour into tray, which has been lined with buttered butcher paper. Let set overnight. In morning, grab butcher paper at both ends and lift carefully. Set on counter and cut into 1-inch squares. This is a creamy fudge. Note: If it begins to dry out, place a piece of bread alongside and cover tightly. It will soften overnight. Makes 15 lbs.

BASQUE FESTIVALS

Nevada's Basque people are proud of their heritage—something that is evident at the Basque festivals held annually in Winnemucca, Elko, Reno, and Las Vegas. The oldest and largest of these celebrations is the National Basque Festival, which is held in Elko on the first weekend in July.

Since 1963, the event has attracted thousands of spectators to enjoy traditional Basque contests, dancing, and food. For example, during the irrintzi competition, participants try to out-do each other in shouting a Basque war cry, and the Basque games include woodchopping and lifting contests.

The following Basque recipes are courtesy of the Zazpiak-Bat Basque Club of Reno, sponsors of the Reno Basque Festival held each August. The recipes originally appeared in *From the Basque Kitchen*, a cookbook published by the club in 1973.

BERAKATZ SOPA
(Garlic Soup)

4 cloves garlic
6 slices bread (cubed and toasted)
3 Tbsp. oil
1 medium can tomatoes or tomato sauce
1/2 bay leaf, crushed
1 tsp. paprika
3 cups water
6 eggs
salt to taste

Heat oil, garlic, and bread in sauce pan. Add boiling water. Add tomato, bay leaf, and paprika. Cook until blended, about 1/2 hour. Stir 6 slightly beaten eggs into soup and cook until eggs thicken. Garnish with minced parsley.

CALAMARES EN SU TINTA
(Squid in Ink Sauce)

5 lbs. frozen calamares (squid) or 4 lbs. if fresh
16 oz. tomato sauce
2 medium onions
1/2 large green pepper
2 cloves garlic
1/2 cup white wine
olive oil

Cleaning calamares is a real chore, but the end product is a gourmet's delight. After removing the head, spiny rod (a long, thin clear bone), eyes, and outer skin, save the tentacles and ink sack. Strain the ink through a fine strainer to separate from the membrane, adding enough water to recover as much ink as possible—about 1/2 cup. Skin the sack and turn inside out, dry with paper towels as well as possible, and stuff the tentacles inside the sack. To make the sauce, brown chopped onion, green pepper, and garlic, then add tomato sauce and ink. Now fry the cleaned calamares in olive oil. Be careful because the oil can splatter. Fry until the squid is golden brown. Add the fried calamares to the sauce and simmer for at least 1 hour (a little longer is better). Add the wine during the last half-hour of cooking. The sauce should be thick.

(Continued)

BASQUE RICE

1 lb. chopped link sausage or homemade Basque sausage
1/2 large onion, chopped
1 clove chopped garlic
1/2 green pepper, chopped
1 4-oz. can mushrooms with juice or use fresh mushrooms
1 2-oz. can pimientos with juice
3 chicken bouillon cubes added to 2-1/2 cups water
1 cup long grain rice
chopped parsley
1 tsp. celery powder
salt and pepper to taste

Brown together the first four ingredients. Do not drain drippings. Add remaining ingredients and simmer slowly for 40 minutes or put in a casserole and bake at 350 degrees for 30 to 40 minutes.

BASQUE POTATOES

3 large potatoes, peeled and sliced
1 cup pimiento, chopped
1 large onion, chopped
1 large clove garlic, put through garlic press
2 Tbsp. olive oil
1 cup chicken broth
2 Tbsp. parsley
salt and pepper to taste

Saute potatoes, onions, and garlic in olive oil for several minutes or until the potatoes are lightly browned. Add pimientos, chicken broth, parsley, salt, and pepper. Simmer slowly until potatoes are soft but not mushy.

ESNE OPILLA
(Basque Caramel Custard)

2 cups whole milk (not 2 percent)
4 large eggs
1/3 cup sugar
1/4 tsp. salt
1/2 tsp. vanilla
For Caramel: 1/2 cup sugar for browning

Preheat oven to 350 degrees. Place 1/2 cup white sugar in bottom of small, deep saucepan, which can later go into the oven. For best results, use a heavy pan. Brown the sugar and coat the sides and the bottom of the pan by tipping it from side to side as the sugar browns and melts. Be careful not to burn the sugar. Whip eggs, milk, 1/3 cup sugar, vanilla, and salt together until foamy. Pour into the carmelized saucepan but do not stir up with caramel. Place saucepan in a larger pan containing 1/2 inch of boiling water, and bake 50 minutes at 350 degrees, or until a knife comes out clean. Let cool and unmold. Melted caramel runs down the sides, forming a sauce. Serves 4.

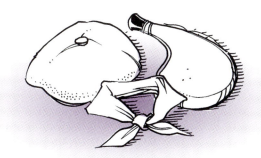

JAPAN FESTIVAL

A mong the newer special events celebrated in Nevada is the Japan Festival, held in November in Las Vegas. Kimono shows, gateball tournaments, karaoke parties, a parade, cultural exhibits, and performances of traditional Japanese plays and music are among the many activities scheduled during the three-day festival.

The following Japanese recipes are courtesy of Hiroko Huffman and the Japan-American Society of Nevada, an organizer of the Japan Festival.

TEMPURA VEGETABLES

1 medium sweet potato
6 mushrooms
2 medium onions
1 small eggplant
2 green peppers
1 carrot

Batter:
2 egg yolks
2 cups ice water
2 cups sifted all purpose flour

Wash the vegetables and cut into bite-sized pieces. Dry thoroughly. Do not make batter ahead of time. Just before using, beat ice water, beaten egg, and flour together, until all ingredients are well moistened (a few lumps are okay). Keep batter cool with a few ice cubes in the batter. Dip vegetables in batter and cook them in deep, hot oil (360 degrees) until tender and browned. Drain thoroughly. Skim off any batter on the surface of the oil. Serves 6 people.

CALIFORNIA ROLLS

1 avocado thinly sliced
3/4 cup imitation crab meat
1 Tbsp. mayonnaise
4-5 sheets of seaweed

Sushi rice:
3 cups short grain rice (raw)
3 cups plus 3 Tbsp. water
6 Tbsp. rice vinegar
3 Tbsp. plus 2-1/4 tsp. sugar
3/4 tsp. salt

Cook rice, but you don't want it soggy. While rice is still hot, pour vinegar and sugar solution into the rice. Mix the rice mixture so that it cools quickly and is less likely to become soggy (it helps to mix it under a ceiling fan). When rice is cool, place seaweed on top of bamboo mats. Spread 3/4 cups of rice over seaweed. Place sliced avocado in a line just off the center of the seaweed/rice base. Place crab mixture next to the avocado. Roll seaweed from the edge, beginning with the edge nearest to you and work toward the center. Cover with the bamboo to make it round. Cut evenly in six pieces, starting at the middle.

RIB COOK-OFFS

Rib cook-offs mean one thing—juicy, succulent pork or beef ribs cooked slowly over an open flame and slathered in a thick, tasty sauce. While there are several rib cook-offs in Nevada, the most prestigious is the Best in the West Nugget Rib Cook-Off, which is held in Sparks in September.

Sponsored by John Ascuaga's Nugget and the city of Sparks, the event attracts 30 top professional and amateur rib cooks in the West, who compete for thousands of dollars in prize money. Spectators can sample the participants' entries during the four-day event, which takes place on Victorian Square. Additionally, the festival offers more than 125 arts and crafts booths and free open-air concerts on four stages.

Since most of the Rib Cook-Off participants are commercial firms, it is difficult to persuade any to share their rib secrets. The following is a recipe for preparing award-winning ribs courtesy of Dennis Ofsthun of Rib Ticklers, the winner of the 1996 cook-off. Rib Ticklers, however, jealously guards its sauce ingredients. The recipe calls for using Rib Ticklers sauce (available at many grocery stores or by calling 1-800-31-8-RIBS) or you can substitute your favorite BBQ sauce.

HOW I WON THE 1996 BEST IN THE WEST NUGGET RIB COOK-OFF

2 cups Rib Ticklers Mild Barbecue Sauce (or sauce of your choice)
1-3/4 cups apple cider vinegar
3/4 cup salad oil
1 tsp. salt
1 tsp. pepper
pork ribs (or beef or chicken), usually figure 1/2 lb. per person
1 cup Rib Ticklers Spicy, Turbo, or Mild Barbecue Sauce
(depending on how hot you want the ribs)

1/2 cup honey
1 cup crushed pineapple
large pan filled with water

Mix 2 cups of Rib Ticklers Mild BBQ sauce with apple cider vinegar, salad oil, salt, and pepper. Marinade pork ribs for 12 to 14 hours in refrigerator. Place ribs in a smoker or covered barbecue with coals off to the side. Place pan of water under meat. Cook for 2 hours at 240 degrees or to 75 percent cooked. Mix 1 cup of Rib Ticklers BBQ sauce (spicy, turbo, or mild) with honey and pineapple. Wrap meat in foil drenched in honey and pineapple sauce. Finish to a tender and moist fall-off-the-bone goodness.

PORTUGUESE FESTAS

Portuguese immigrants have played an important role in the development of Nevada. Several communities, including Yerington, Lovelock, and Fallon, host annual Portuguese Festas to celebrate the state's rich Portuguese history and culture. In addition to parades, crafts shows, dancing exhibitions, and music, the events often feature a Portuguese dinner, which includes a traditional dish called sopas (beef stew).

The first recipe is courtesy of the United Portuguese of the State of California, Carson City Council. The second recipe is courtesy of Elsie Brower and the Yerington Portuguese Organization, sponsor of the Yerington Portuguese Celebration, held in May.

PORTUGUESE SOPAS

5 lbs. chuck roast
1 can tomato sauce
1/2 medium onion, chopped fine
1/2 tsp. black pepper
1 tsp. salt
1 cup burgundy wine or 1/4 cup vinegar
1 cup water
1/4 cup catsup
1/4 tsp. garlic salt
1/2 tsp. whole cloves
1/4 tsp. whole cumin seed
1/2 tsp. whole allspice
3 or 4 bay leaves
1 stick cinnamon
sprigs of mint
French bread

Put the roast in a heavy roaster (one with a lid) and place tomato sauce, onions, pepper, salt, wine, water, catsup, and garlic salt around the roast. Put the remaining ingredients (cloves, cumin seed, allspice, bay leaves, and cinnamon) in a tea strainer or wrap in cheesecloth. Put container with spices down into the juice. Cover roaster and cook for 3 to 3-1/2 hours at 350 degrees. When cooked, remove pan from heat and let cool so that all fat will come to the top of the pan. Remove fat, then add 1-1/2 to 2 quarts water (to suite taste). Simmer with meat for 30 minutes or so. Pour juice over mint and sliced French bread. Serve meat in separate bowl. Do not forget to serve with dill pickles.

FESTA POTATO SALAD

6-8 potatoes, boiled with skins on
4-5 hard boiled eggs
6 green onions, finely chopped
4 stalks celery, finely chopped
1/2 bunch fresh parsley, finely chopped
1 small jar pimientos, drained and chopped
2 heaping Tbsps. sweet pickle relish
1-2 cups mayonaisse
salt to taste

Peel cooked, cooled potatoes. Dice into 1-inch cubes. Coarsely chop peeled eggs and add to potatoes. Mix in chopped celery, green onions, parsley, pimiento, and relish. Add mayonaisse and salt to taste. Mix well and chill for at least 3 hours. Garnish with paprika or sliced hard boiled eggs (optional). Serves 12 people.

CRANBERRY FESTIVAL

One of the Las Vegas area's most intriguing food events is the annual Cranberry Festival. The idea of blending cranberries—which only grow in wet climates—with dry Las Vegas might seem bizarre but for the fact that the Ocean Spray Cranberry World West attraction is located in Henderson, a suburb of Las Vegas.

Cranberry World West contains exhibits describing cranberry growing, harvesting, and processing. The center also has a gift shop, a juice bar where guests can taste as many as 10 flavors of Ocean Spray cranberry juice blends, and a demonstration kitchen, which tests new recipes that use Ocean Spray products.

The Cranberry Festival, which is held in September, is sponsored by Cranberry World West and is a celebration of all things cranberry. The event includes a parade, recipe contest, crafts, carnival rides, and entertainment.

The following recipe is courtesy of Ocean Spray Cranberry World West.

ORIENTAL CHICKEN SALAD

5 oz. dried Chinese noodles
3 Tbsp. olive oil
2 Tbsp. frozen orange juice concentrate, thawed
1 tsp. coarsely ground pepper
3/4 tsp. garlic powder
1/4 tsp. ginger
1 6-oz. package of Craisins (sweetened, dried cranberries)
1 11-oz. can mandarin oranges, drained
3 green onions, white and green parts, sliced
1 lb. chicken tenders
2-3 Tbsp. poppy seeds
2 Tbsp. oil

Cook noodles (without flavor packet, if included) according to package directions. Rinse with cold water; drain thoroughly. Set aside. Combine olive oil, orange juice concentrate, pepper, garlic powder, and ginger, mixing vigorously with a fork. Add to noodles, tossing to mix. Gently toss in dried cranberries, oranges, and green onions. Place in serving bowl; set aside. Rinse chicken with cool water; pat dry. Sprinkle poppy seeds on a plate. Press one side of each chicken tender into poppy seeds. Heat oil in a medium frying pan. Place chicken, poppy seed side down, in the pan. Cook until chicken is no longer pink inside, about 5 minutes, turning only once. Place chicken on top of noodles. Makes 3 servings.

NOTES